Three Wisconsin

A sketch of the lives of Howard B., Alonzo H. and William B.
Cushing, children of a pioneer family of Waukesha County

Theron Wilber Haight

Alpha Editions

This edition published in 2023

ISBN : 9789357932684

Design and Setting By
Alpha Editions
www.alphaedis.com
Email - info@alphaedis.com

RECORDS AND APPRECIATIONS

Howard B. Cushing

Record—Wisconsin. Private Co. B., 1st Illinois artillery, March 24, 1862 to November 30, 1863; private in B artillery (regular) November 30, 1863; second lieutenant, 4th artillery, November 30, 1863; transferred to 3rd cavalry, September 7, 1867; first lieutenant, December 16, 1867; killed May 5, 1871, in action with Apache Indians in Whetstone Mountains, Arizona.

Appreciation—"Of the distinguished services rendered to Arizona by Lieutenant Howard B. Cushing, a book might well be written. It is not intended to disparage anybody when I say that he performed herculean and more notable work, perhaps, than had been performed by any other officer of corresponding rank either before or since. Southern Arizona owed much to the gallant officers who wore out strength and freely risked life and limb in her defence; * * * but if there were any choice among them I am sure that the verdict, if left to those officers themselves, would be in favor of Cushing."—JOHN G. BOURKE, *On the Border with Crook* (N. Y., 1891), pp. 106, 107.

Alonzo Hersford Cushing

Record—Wisconsin and New York. Cadet at Military Academy, July 1, 1857 (12); second lieutenant and first lieutenant of the 4th artillery, June 24, 1861; brevet captain, December 13, 1862, for gallant and meritorious service at the battle of Fredericksburg, Va.; major, May 2, 1862, for gallant and meritorious service at the Battle of Chancellorsville, Va.; and lieutenant colonel, July 1, 1863, for conspicuous gallantry at the Battle of Gettysburg, Pa., where he was killed July 3, 1863.

Appreciation—"On the field of Gettysburg, more than once I stood where the brave Cushing gave up his life, right at the peak of Pickett's daring charge. Oh that day and that hour! History will not let that smiling, splendid boy die in vain; her dew will glisten forever over his record as the earthly morning dew glistens in the fields. Fame loves the gentleman and the true-hearted, but her sweetheart is gallant youth."—MORRIS SCHAFF, "Spirit of Old West Point," in *Atlantic Monthly*, February, 1907.

William Barker Cushing

Record—September 25, 1857, appointed acting midshipman, from 33rd N. Y. district; March 23, 1861, resignation accepted; April 1, appointed master's mate in volunteer navy—served on board the U. S. S. "Minnesota;" Sept. 13, resignation accepted; Oct. 19, warranted as a midshipman in the navy from the 1st day of June, 1861; Oct. 25, to duty in North Atlantic blockading squadron; March 27, 1862, detached from U. S. S. "Cambridge" (sick) and leave of one month; May 14, to the U. S. S. "Minnesota;" July 16, promoted to lieutenant; April 27, 1863, commissioned; Sept. 5, detached from the "Shockokon" and to command the "Monticello;" Oct. 19, 1864, detached and to the North Atlantic blockading squadron; Nov. 22, again ordered to North Atlantic blockading squadron; Oct. 27, promoted to lieutenant-commander from this date; Feb. 20, 1865, commissioned; Feb. 24, detached from command of the "Monticello" and wait orders; May 17, to the navy yard, New York, N. Y.; June 13, detached and to the U. S. S. "Hartford;" June 24, detached and to the U. S. S. "Lancaster," Pacific station; March 11, 1867, detached and wait orders; July 5, to the U. S. S. "Quinnebaug," 15th instant; July 25, previous order revoked and to command the U. S. S. "Penobscot" when found; Oct. 7, detached and to command the U. S. S. "Maumee;" Jan. 19, 1870, detached November 12th last, and leave three months from 13th instant; March 30, to ordnance duty, Navy Yard, Boston, Mass., April 30th; Jan. 31, 1872, promoted to commander from this date; Feb. 2, to examination; Feb. 9, detached and wait orders; May 16, commissioned; June 17, 1873, to command the U. S. S. "Wyoming" per steamer 28th instant; June 21, previous order suspended; July 11, to command the U. S. S. "Wyoming;" April 24, 1874, detached and wait orders; April 27, to duty as assistant to executive officer, Navy Yard, Washington, D. C.; Aug. 25, detached and to duty as senior aid to commandant of the Navy Yard, Washington, D. C.; Dec. 17, died this day at the Government Hospital for the Insane, Washington, D. C.

Appreciation—"To the Senate and House of Representatives: In conformity to the law of July 16, 1862, I most cordially recommend that Lieutenant William B. Cushing, United States Navy, receive a vote of thanks from Congress for his important, gallant, and perilous achievement in destroying the rebel ironclad steamer, Albemarle, on the night of the 27th of October, 1864, at Plymouth, North Carolina. * * * This recommendation is specially made in order to comply with the requirements of the aforesaid act which is in the following words, viz.: That any line officer of the Navy or Marine Corps may be advanced one grade if upon recommendation of the President by name he receives the thanks of Congress for highly distinguished conduct in conflict with the enemy, or for extraordinary heroism in the lines of his profession. (Signed)

ABRAHAM LINCOLN."

THREE WISCONSIN CUSHINGS

A Great New England Exodus

Beginning with the last decade of the eighteenth century, and continuing through the first decade of the nineteenth, the northern and western borders of the state of New York were punctuated with settlements of a peculiar people along the entire distance, and reaching inland from the edges of the lakes and rivers along the line, for a number of miles. These settlements were from New England; but their population differed somewhat from the aggregate of those who were left behind. Sires and sons of the great emigration were, in all their movements, much influenced, no doubt, by the views of their wives, mothers, and sisters, but the partiality of history takes notice only of the former.

They were the men, and the offspring of the men, whose sturdy strokes, supplemented by their more delicate and elaborate strokes, had turned New England from a wilderness into fertile fields and flourishing towns, but who were not permitted to reap the fruits of their past endeavors in their old homes. Debts had accrued against them while they had been helping fight the battles of their country in the War for Independence, and their creditors would not accept in settlement the worthless Continental currency with which their country had paid them for their services and sacrifices. In many instances they found their homesteads taken from them and turned over to lawyers and other professional men who had abstained from encouragement of bloodshed by staying out of the army in the "times that tried men's souls." The returning soldiers were disgusted and amazed by what looked to them like a less tolerable condition than that which they had opposed of late with powder and ball. Within a very few years all this feeling culminated in a rebellion against the government—and particularly the judicial branch of the government—of the state of Massachusetts, led by one Daniel Shays, who had attained the rank of captain in the Continental forces in active service.

When this uprising was suppressed, as in less than a year it was, an exodus of the dissatisfied classes began and continued as people could get ready for their passage over the Hudson and into the wilderness of what was then the Far West, reaching by way of the Mohawk Valley even to Lake Erie itself, and up the eastern shore of Lake Ontario to the St. Lawrence. Washington Irving was evidently familiar with the appearance of such migrations from early boyhood, and gives a lively picture in his *Knickerbocker's History of New York* (though somewhat distorted for purposes of burlesque entertainment), of the way in which the Yankees moved westward, accompanied by their families, and with all their belongings packed away in covered wagons drawn by jaded horses or toiling oxen.

The History was published in 1809, when Irving was twenty-six years old; but it is not probable that he had observed among the immigrant wagons passing his father's house, the young ship-carpenter, Zattu Cushing, who attained his majority in 1791, and soon after left his native home at Plymouth, Mass., reaching the neighborhood of Ballston Spa, New York, before 1795, the year of his marriage there to Miss Rachel Buckingham.

It seems most likely that the trip from Plymouth to the headwaters of the Hudson was entirely by water; the young man's relations with seafaring, together with the frequency of coastwise voyages from the eastern ports of the old Bay State, would naturally have led him to prefer that route. From the time of his marriage until 1799 neither tradition nor record points out the character or direction of his movements. In the last-mentioned year he is said to have been superintending the construction of a ship, the "Good Intent," at the island opposite Erie, Pennsylvania, although his residence at the same time was in the town of Paris, a few miles south of Utica, New York. On his return home from Erie he took back a team of horses, perhaps the fruit of his ship-building on the lake. The horses claim a a place in history on account of the escape of one of them in the neighborhood of Dunkirk, and the camping-out of the owner, while searching for it, on the site of the village of Fredonia, his home in subsequent years.

The Cushing Family in Western New York

It was not until 1805 that the young man finally settled at Fredonia, bringing with him his wife and five children, of whom Milton Buckingham, born in 1800, was to become the father of perhaps the most conspicuously daring trio of sons of one mother of any—not excepting the Roman Horatii or Judean Maccabees—whose exploits have been noted in the pages of history. For, in the days of early champions, personal strength and dexterity counted for so much in battle that it did not appear very extraordinary for Walter Scott's "Fitz-James" to set his back against a rock and defy a whole tribe of armed Highlanders to a close contest. The more modern fighting man can not see the death that he hears whistling and humming about his head in the vicious flight of bullets; or, tearing the atmosphere apart by means of shell that burst into whirring fragments of cast-iron, destroying everything they touch, whether animate or inanimate. He has to be ready for his fate, which may be handed out to him at any instant without the possibility of resistance or escape.

The journey from Oneida County was made in the early winter by ox-sleighs, and must have taken several days, perhaps running into weeks, as the route led the emigrants to Dunkirk by way of Buffalo and the frozen waters along the Erie shore. While spending one night on the ice, a little way off shore, a thaw came on, in company with a strong east wind, and the party had some difficulty in reaching land. Fredonia is only three or four miles inland from the port of Dunkirk, and the family soon found themselves domiciled in the log hut which in those days almost always served as the temporary shelter, at least, of the first occupant of a tract of land in the backwoods of New York.

The Cushings were evidently well-thought-of by their neighbors, so the former ship-carpenter soon received the appointment of associate judge of the Niagara County court. It may seem rather odd at present that this position should have been conferred upon a layman; but the experience at their old homes of the emigrating New Englanders had been such that they retained strong prejudices against regularly-trained members of the learned professions. They were quite generally inclined to prefer the illiterate exhortations of revivalist ministers to the teachings of such clergymen as were accounted orthodox in the Eastern states; to consider home-bred lawyers as more likely to strive for the triumph of justice than those who had devoted their lives to the study of technicalities; and even in respect to medical practitioners, the self-taught empiric was as likely to achieve a financial success among them as would be the graduate of a long-established medical school.

That the choice of Mr. Cushing as a judge was approved by the people, became evident when Chautauqua County was set off from Niagara. In 1811, Judge Cushing took the place of presiding judge in the new organization, and held it for fourteen years. In 1826, after the opening of the Erie Canal, the judge, in company with other citizens of Fredonia, built a boat for traffic on the new waterway, and had it hauled over the three miles between Fredonia and the lake, by ox-teams; there were said to have been about a hundred in the string. The jurist therefore did not retire from the activities of life on retiring from the bench; he found somewhat with which to occupy himself until his death in 1839, respected and honored by the community where he lived.

The Father of Three Wisconsin Heroes

In the meantime his son Milton had grown to maturity, had taken the degree of doctor of medicine after a classical course of study at Hamilton Literary and Theological Institute, not far from the early boyhood home of the student—a school founded in 1820, and now become Colgate University. The duties of a physician were too exacting for his own health, however.

After a few years of practice at Zanesville, Ohio, where he married his first wife, he became a local merchant, and in 1833, when the wife died, was the father of four children, none of whom long survived their early manhood or womanhood.

Not long after the death of Mrs. Cushing, Dr. Cushing removed his business and home to Columbus, where in 1836 he married Miss Mary Barker Smith of Boston, who was visiting in the West at the time. She was then 29 years old, of splendid physical and mental constitution, and fortunately endowed with a passionate love for life in an open, free atmosphere, as near as practicable to nature itself.

After the birth of their eldest son, named for his father, in 1837, the young couple prepared for their removal into the far west of Wisconsin, where the Potawatomi still fished and hunted, and whence the Sauk leader, Black Hawk, had recently been driven. Neither documentary evidence nor tradition show the manner of travel of the young couple—whether through the prairies of Indiana and Illinois, and down the east shore of Lake Michigan, or by sailing vessel around through the straits of Mackinac. Either of the two routes was then available, and neither was especially dangerous.

What seems certain is, that on the 22nd of August, 1838, Howard B. Cushing, the eldest of the three Wisconsin-born members of that family, first saw the light at Milwaukee. Nine days previous to the event, Mrs. Cushing was impressed with the presentiment of death, and wrote in her Bible the verses following, under the heading, "To Milton, with the Legacy of his Mother's Bible."[1]

[1] E. M. H. Edwards, *Commander William Barker Cushing* (N. Y., 1898), pp. 22, 23.

I have no gold, my darling son,
No wealth to leave to thee—
Yet never light hath shone upon
A richer, costlier, holier one
Than this my legacy;
"Bought with a price," this guide of youth—
And gemmed with wisdom, light, and truth.

Should'st thou live on through many years,
Of pilgrimage below,
Full well I know that earthly fears
And human woe and human tears,
Attend the path thou'lt go,

And that thy soul may well endure—
Drink deeply of this fountain pure.

Farewell, my son! perchance through grace
We'll meet again above—
Thine infant memory may not trace
Thy mother's form, thy mother's face;
But O, that mother's love
Burns deep for thee, my first-born child!
God keep thy spirit undefiled!

If this is to be understood as an indication of despondent gloom, on the part of the writer, it is the only one left by this conspicuous exemplar of fine American womanhood. In later years, as will appear in these pages, she was obliged to undergo privations more difficult to encounter than those of a residence at the confluence of the Milwaukee and Menomonee rivers—then a forlorn waste of swamps and hills, that looked as though they would successfully defy the efforts of man for transformation into the fairest of the cities along the shores of the Great Lakes.

In 1838 the little village contained not more than about eight hundred inhabitants, and these were divided by Milwaukee River into two hostile camps, whose differences were always apparently on the point of breaking out into actual violence. The stream was still unbridged, and it seemed likely that this watery frontier would long remain a boundary line as fixed as that of the Rhine in Europe. Mrs. Cushing had been reared among the most highly-cultivated people of Boston, and was related to such distinguished families as the Adamses, Hancocks, and Phillipses. It was not at all strange, therefore, that with three or four children of her husband by a former wife to care for, besides her own baby of sixteen months, she should have been attacked by the nostalgia that has often dragged grown men to untimely graves.

It was an evidence of the strength of character of this city-bred lady that she so soon recovered her elasticity of spirit after the birth of Howard, and again faced the hardships of frontier life as fearlessly as her sons faced death in the campaigns of the great Civil War. It must have been soon after her convalescence that she paralleled the shout of Hannibal's soldiers, "Beyond the Alps lies Italy!" with the thought, at least, that beyond the Menomonee marshes lay a country resembling in aspect the most carefully tended English parks, but swarming with more delicious and satisfying game of earth, water, and air than could be found in any open hunting grounds of Europe. This was the country of the "oak openings," extending for scores of miles to the westward, and jeweled with lovely lakelets, from Pewaukee to beyond the

"Four Lakes," between two of which latter was to rise the capital of the nascent state.

From Milwaukee to the Nemahbins

In 1838 there was no elaborate road between Milwaukee and Waukesha, but the intervening twenty miles presented no serious obstacles to travel. A pioneer woman who made the trip that year, Mrs. Talbot C. Dousman, wrote of it[2] that her pen was inadequate to a description of the beautiful scenes. The prairie grasses stood as high as the horses' knees, and thick with lovely flowers. Often, says she, "we found ourselves looking about for the house belonging to these beautiful grounds; but it was emphatically 'God's country,' without sight or sound of human habitation, from the house where we dined [in the present town of Brookfield] till we reached our home in the woods, thirty miles from Milwaukee."

[2] *History of Waukesha County, Wis.* (Chicago, 1880), pp. 473, 474.

The route taken by the Paddock family, and thus depicted by one of its daughters, passed the site of Waukesha rather more than a mile north, and ended not far from the subsequent home of the Cushings. Indeed, it was most probably followed by the Cushings early in 1839, and one may feel no hesitation in believing that the latter breathed in with delight the clear, sweet atmosphere of the "openings," as they passed from hill to hill, skirting the south shore of Pewaukee Lake and the southern point of Nagawicka, under the shadow of the magnificent semi-mountain of Wisconsin's Kettle Range, and then into the charming valley surrounded by lakelets and now occupied by the beautiful little village of Delafield.

At that time there was no obstruction to the free flowage of Bark River from Nagawicka to the upper Nemahbin, two miles to the westward. The site of the log cabin chosen by Dr. Cushing is about half way between those lakes, and only a few rods north of the river. It may still be recognized by travellers on the interurban trolley, by means of two beautiful elm trees across the river, from a point half a mile west of the trolley station at Delafield. Less than a mile farther north, are the buildings of the Nashotah Theological Seminary, some of which are also visible from the electric road. Then, however, oak openings extended north and south without visible termination. It was an ideal place for rest from the busy employments of the world, and Mrs. Cushing long afterwards said that her sojourn there was the happiest period of her life.

Almost immediately, Dr. Cushing took a prominent place in this community. Appointed justice of the peace, he made the first entries in his docket February 15, 1840, in a case tried before him, between G. S. Hosmer, plaintiff, and Russell Frisby, defendant. What is now the township of Delafield was then the south half of the town of Warren, but it was the next winter set off by an act of the legislature under the name of Nemahbin, and Dr. Cushing was placed at the head of the new municipal organization as chairman of its first board of supervisors. The town meeting at which he was elected was held January 5, 1842, at the schoolhouse; and over it presided George Paddock, whom we have already noted as guiding his daughter to this locality.

More than two years before, on December 28, 1839, a second son had been born to Mrs. Cushing and her husband, and named Walter. The date of the death of this child is not preserved, but he could not have outlived very early childhood, since the burial place was on the farm from which the parents removed within the next five years.

Alonzo was also born on the Delafield farm, as shown by a family Bible lately brought to light. Until this discovery his birth had been credited to Milwaukee, like that of his elder brother, Howard. He was born on January 19, 1841.

Neither store nor post office had yet been established in the little hamlet, nor was either of those conveniences to be found there for more than two years afterward. The original Hawks's tavern was built and opened to the public in 1840, and was deemed a great blessing by immigrants on their way westward along the lately-cleared Territorial Road; but there were no table supplies to be found on sale nearer than Prairieville (now Waukesha), a dozen miles back towards Milwaukee.

The year 1842 was an eventful one for the frontier township of Nemahbin, since in the early part of the summer, a milldam was built at the outlet of Nagawicka Lake, while not long after a gentleman named Delafield arrived there, purchased the water power and its improvements, and erected a flouring mill where the village mill has ever since been a conspicuous figure in the landscape. But of far greater importance was the birth, in the cabin north of the river of which we have already spoken, on November 4, of that later glory of the American navy, William Barker Cushing.

As Dr. Cushing's first wife died in 1833, it follows that the youngest of her children could not have been at this time less than nine years old. Although nothing is told of the date of the former marriage in any writings accessible to me, it seems likely that the eldest of the children of that connection may have been born as early as 1825, and therefore may have become fairly well qualified to take charge of the household during any temporary incapacity on the part of Mrs. Cushing herself.

Mrs. Edwards states in her life of the naval commander[3] that there were four children of Dr. Cushing's first marriage, but gives the names of only three of them, who were all members of the family in Wisconsin. The Milwaukee County records show the purchase, in 1844, by Mrs. Cushing from Dr. Castleman, to whom the farm had then been sold, of a burial lot, 6 feet by 4, including a grave, undoubtedly that of her third son, Walter; and William was the youngest of her sons and the youngest of the family except a daughter, born in Chicago and still living there—Mrs. Isabel Cushing Bouton. In Mrs. Edwards' volume, however, Mrs. Cushing is credited with being the mother of seven, though she names only five. The last conveyance by Dr. Cushing himself appearing in the register's office at Waukesha, is a deed to Dr. Castleman of part of his holdings, dated April 13, 1843. It may be pretty safely assumed that he became aware at about that time of the inroads of a disease in his own system which some four years later proved fatal.

[3] Edwards, op. cit., p. 15.

Removal to Chicago

In 1844, then, it is probable that the wife and mother left the little town that she had learned to love so well, and wended her way to Chicago with her own children and those of her husband's former marriage. It is said that she had suggested the name of Delafield for the township, because the Nemahbin lakes were not within its boundaries. The change in designation was made by the legislature in 1843. During all the time of the residence of the family here, they lived in Milwaukee County, in the Territory of Wisconsin. Waukesha County had not yet been accorded a separate civic organization, and Wisconsin did not become a state until 1848. Mrs. Cushing's choice for the name of the place was stated by her to have been influenced by what she considered the more euphonious sound of the name adopted, when compared with the family name that was to be immortalized and made resplendent by her three sons born in Wisconsin. It is a pity that the town had not been called Cushing, for Mr. Delafield died soon afterwards, and the mill property was sold with the rest of the estate of the deceased in 1846, since which date there has been nothing of an historical character to remind one of the origin of the local name.

There is no available information of the events of the three years ending with 1847 and relating to the Cushing family in Chicago—a town not then as satisfactory from an aesthetic view-point as the Milwaukee they had left in 1839. Perhaps an exception should be made to this statement of lack of information, in favor of an anecdote told by Mrs. Edwards of the young William walking off into Lake Michigan, and informing his rescuer that his name was "Bill Coon," so that he could not be immediately identified. He consequently was lost to his family for the succeeding thirty-six hours. It is also mentioned incidentally that Dr. Cushing resumed the practice of medicine at Chicago, but he could hardly have attained much success in it, on account of his declining health. Early in 1847 he returned to Ohio, perhaps arranging there for the future of the two sons by his first marriage, one of whom became a lawyer and partner of Salmon P. Chase, and the other a physician; but both died several years before the outbreak of the war.

The Mother in Charge of the Family

Dr. Cushing himself died at Gallipolis, Ohio, on April 22, 1847. He must have been a man of considerable force of character, and of great personal attractiveness, as well as of correct conceptions of right and wrong, with sympathies always for the right side of public questions. His physical constitution was not robust, however, and he therefore passed away without leaving any memory of important action of his own, and without provision for his widow and her children.

It is at this point that Mrs. Cushing's personality becomes more distinctly visible to the investigator of the family annals. Having to lay out a course of life with particular reference to the welfare of her little ones, she wisely decided, like Ruth in the ancient story, to go back to the home of her husband's relatives, and there to begin life anew. She loved her independence and had no intention of quartering herself upon the charity of those well-disposed people; but it was reasonable to hope that they, or some of them, would take sufficient interest in the boys, at any rate, to point out ways and means for their development into good citizens, and opportunities of which they might take advantage to win places of honor and usefulness among their fellow men.

She was very soon enabled to establish a school for children at Fredonia, by means of which, with the practice of strict economy, she maintained her family in a respectable manner. The indulgence of social vanities was of course not within the scope of her plans. Her boys were required to help in the support of the family by the performance of such slight tasks as the neighbors called upon them to accomplish—driving cows to pasture, and other "chores" of a similar character. All moneys earned by this work were handed over to the mother and employed to the common advantage of the family. Mrs. Bouton, of Chicago, the youngest of the children, and the only one now surviving, writes this, of her early life at home:

One trait, I think, was very remarkable in our family—the respect and courtesy manifested toward each other. I never received a reproof or heard an impatient word from either of my brothers. They always displayed toward each other and my mother and myself, the same courtesy they would show to a commanding officer. The petting and love I received was enough to have spoiled me for life for contact with the world.

In the case of William, at least, the spirit of courtesy would not appear to have been so overwhelming as to prevent an occasional exuberance of spirits, an instance of which is told of in a letter from Mrs. Julia G. Horton of Buffalo, cited by Mrs. Edwards as follows:[4]

[4] Ibid, p. 38.

Will was never happier than when playing some joke upon one of his elder brothers. One summer evening I accompanied his brother Alonzo (Allie, as we used to call him) "to the mill-pond," upon his invitation to take a row in a forlorn old scow which was much patronized by the young people for what they considered delightful trips over the smooth pond. When we reached the bank we found that some one had untied the boat and set it adrift. No other boat was to be had and so we sat down on a log, wondering if some one had tricked us out of our row. Soon we heard a wild whoop in the distance and saw Master Will waving an oar and shouting to us: "Next time you want to row, don't forget to ask your friends."

Mrs. Horton also tells an anecdote of how the future commander followed her and one of his brothers to a prayer-meeting, seating himself behind them and singing improvised personalities instead of the approved words of the hymns that were being sung by the worshippers, so that he was discovered by a church official and led out of the congregation in disgrace. There are other like narratives surviving among the relatives and acquaintances of the Cushings, but none of them throw additional light upon the young men in whom we are at this time most interested. With Milton, the eldest, tradition has not seemed to busy itself. He was not a native of Wisconsin; and it may be enough to say here that in due time he became a paymaster in the Union navy, receiving promotion, until he was retired for disability, as paymaster of the fleet then in the Mediterranean, and died January 1, 1886. He married, but left no issue.

Of the younger lads, Howard appears to have been endowed with an unusual aspiration for independence of action, so that at fourteen years of age he took the position of "devil" in the office of *The Censor*, in his home village of

Fredonia. As soon as he had obtained enough of the technique of the trade to imagine himself able to hold his own among strangers, he went to Boston, where flourished the aristocratic relatives of his mother. Here he continued his labors at the press and in the composing room until affected with some illness that made him homesick as well, upon which he returned to Fredonia to recover under his mother's ministrations. When that result was attained he started for Chicago, memories of which progressive town doubtless had haunted him all through his sojourn in the East.

He had left Chicago before he was ten years old. The Cushing traits of character were shared by him in such measure, however, as to make it reasonably certain that he was remembered affectionately by former acquaintances, and the road towards independence was doubtless made as easy for him as it could be made with a youth whose dread of being under personal obligations to his friends was in any instance hard to overcome. A situation as typesetter was given him in the office of *The Farmer's Advocate*, and in that capacity and place he worked until his enlistment in 1862 as a private soldier in an Illinois volunteer artillery regiment.

All the Boys Established

In the meantime, Alonzo was bravely attending to such home duties as would be valuable in lightening his mother's work.

In 1855 her brother-in-law, Francis S. Edwards, took his seat as member of Congress from the Thirty-fourth New York district, and the next year procured the appointment of William as a page on the floor of the House.

Towards the end of the session he also secured the appointment of Alonzo as a cadet at West Point, where he entered in 1857, in the seventeenth year of his age, being described in the Academy records as 5 feet and 5 inches tall.

William was then fourteen, and a favorite among the congressmen with whom he came into touch. He also attracted the notice of a relative, Commodore Joseph Smith of the Navy, afterwards admiral, who took measures to have the boy entered as a cadet at the Naval Academy at Annapolis.

Milton was employed in a pharmacy at Fitchburg, Mass., where he remained until the outbreak of the war.

Mrs. Cushing henceforth had only herself and her young daughter to provide for. She had fought a good fight, and had succeeded in the establishment of all her sons in positions in which they were tolerably well assured of a good equipment for life work, in which the ordinary young American of that era only needed a sound mind in a sound body and a fair field, with no favor, in order to accomplish something worth while, whether in war or in peace.

But it should be here noted, that the all-important feature of personal character was and is requisite in the making of an American whose existence is to be of advantage to his country. In such a republic as ours, the nation would surely fail of long endurance if a considerable proportion of its citizens did not hold the national welfare as something higher and more sacred than that of their own individual personality, and could not be found able and willing when the emergency should arise, to give their best efforts, even at the imminent peril of life and limb, to the advancement of the common welfare. It was the prevalence of such elements of character among great numbers of our citizens that carried us through the stress of the Civil War in a manner that left us afterwards stronger and more respected by the whole world than before its beginning, and which now bids fair to place us beyond dispute at the head of all the nations of the earth. In the building up of character of this kind, women were most potent, and among American women Mary Cushing stands in this respect in the very front rank. This was evidenced by her furnishing to the country in its day of need at least three youthful sons so equipped in intellect, nerve, and unflinching will as to be among the most serviceable of all the soldiers and sailors of the Union army and navy.

The four years following the entrance of Alonzo and William to the military and naval academies respectively, were devoid of any incidents of absorbing interest in the lives of the young Cushings. At West Point, Alonzo was approved by his superiors and beloved by his fellows. Modest in demeanor, but always efficient in his work, and kindly towards under-classmen, General Morris Schaff's "Spirit of Old West Point"[5] shows the esteem in which he was held by all. He was graduated June 24, 1861, and on the same day commissioned second lieutenant in the Fourth Artillery, being promoted to first lieutenant before leaving the hall.

[5] *Atlantic Monthly*, February, 1907.

William's cadet experience was somewhat more eventful, for the reason that the spirit of mischief was more dominant with him at that time than with his brothers. The culmination of his pranks was reached towards the close of the winter of 1861, when he fixed a bucket of water at the top of the doorway through which his teacher of Spanish was to pass on his way to an evening party. The teacher was deluged, but the youngster was given permission to resign his cadetship, which he did on March 23. This release was necessary for the sake of discipline, but it was evidently not the intention of the officers to allow him to pass permanently out of the navy. In a month after his enforced resignation he was acting master's mate on board the frigate

"Minnesota," from which he wrote a letter dated May 7, 1861, to his cousin, Miss Mary B. Edwards, at East Troy, Wisconsin, that may serve to indicate his feeling as to his chosen profession at the beginning of its really serious work. He says:

I can write but a few hasty lines. I am an officer on board of the splendid steam frigate, Minnesota. We have just left our moorings, and as I write, we are moving under steam and sail, out of Boston harbor. I am going to fight under the old banner of freedom. I may never return, but if I die it shall be under the folds of the flag that sheltered my infancy, and while striking a blow for its honor and my own. * * * Wherever there is fighting, there we will be, and where there is danger in the battle, there will I be, for I will gain a name in this war. I must now say, Good-by; God bless you, Mary. I will write you from homeward bound vessels as often as possible.

The young lady to whom this and many other letters were written by William B. Cushing, during his stay at Annapolis and subsequently, was a daughter of the congressman who took the boy to Washington in the first instance, and it is likely that the two young people were on terms of familiar acquaintance with each other while they were at the capital. He writes to her as though she were his confidential friend as well as his cousin. Seven weeks after sending the foregoing he wrote again from the "Colorado," that he had

been to the North twice in command of valuable prize ships captured from the enemy. I am now on my return trip from one of these expeditions. One of my prizes was worth seventy-five thousand dollars, while the last was nearly double in value to that. I have gained considerable honor by taking them safely to New York and Philadelphia, and I expect promotion before long.

His expectation proved well grounded, although in a boy of eighteen it may have seemed rather extravagant. Before completing his twentieth year, as will appear later, he had the unique distinction (for one of his age) of being given absolute command of one of the Union gunboats. But that story will properly wait.

The Beginning of the War

From another account it seems that one of the prizes, "The Delaware Farmer," was taken in by Cushing himself, and was the first taken in the war by anybody. During most of July the young sailor was on duty with the blockading squadron off the coast of the Carolinas. In August he was once more on the waters of the Chesapeake, engaged in storming a land battery and destroying some small supporting vessels at the same place. In the meantime, Alonzo was just as rapidly obtaining distinction. From West Point he had proceeded without delay to Washington, and on reaching the capital had applied himself most assiduously to the work most necessary at that time to be performed. When the writer of this sketch arrived at Washington as a member of a volunteer regiment early in July, 1861, Alonzo's smooth, swarthy face and supple figure were to be seen wherever there was a volunteer battery in need of instruction and drill. Although he worked his pupils hard, they all loved him for his radiant smiles and frequent infectious laughter, which were potent factors in smoothing the grim front of grizzled war.

He was then only in his twenty-first year and looked still younger. Standing 5 ft. 9 in. in his stockings, his length of limb was such as to give him the appearance, when on horseback, of being under middle height. His good nature was so unusual on the part of young regular officers, that it captivated every volunteer with whom he came in contact. On July 18 he was at the front in the battle, or rather reconnaissance, at Blackburn's Ford, near the stone bridge over Bull Run, and three days later was in the thick of the disastrous fight on the farther side of that stream. His conduct on that occasion was said to have been admirable, but his position was not yet sufficiently advanced to secure him mention in the reports of general officers, such as became a mere matter of course as soon as he fought on his own responsibility, whether in command of his battery or detached for important staff duty at corps and grand division headquarters.

In no instance is there record of failure on his part to meet the utmost expectations of his superior officers, while generally he exceeded those expectations by a great margin. Although not at the very head of his class at the Military Academy, all who knew him concur in the opinion that he came as near realizing the ideal of a perfect soldier as any of the contestants of the Civil War. His assignment to duty as a first lieutenant of artillery on leaving the Academy, was strong proof that high expectations were already formed as to his future.

Within less than a month after he left West Point (July 22, 1861, to be specific), in company with some thousands of other infantry soldiers, I was floundering along the vile wagon way from the Long Bridge to Bailey's Cross Roads, where our regiment was to make its headquarters for several weeks afterwards, sending out scouting parties from time to time, and establishing picket outposts in what appeared to our uneducated eyes to be appropriate points of vantage. On the Monday just mentioned, a copious rain set in at a very early hour, and the roadsides were strewn with knapsacks, blankets, and other impedimenta of the returning soldiers who plodded along towards Washington from the battle of the day before. Many of them had marched all night, and very few of them had taken more than short intervals of rest during their night exit from the vicinity of Bull Run. One battery was distinguished for its fine appearance, however; and that was Battery A of the Fourth regular artillery. Cushing was in command of it when it met and passed us, and even the events of the preceding twenty-four hours had not been sufficient to take away his smile—although it might have shown a sarcastic side to a closer observer than I then was.

The infantry regiment in which I was a private retired to Arlington, about the first of September, from the front line of the troops around Washington, and found that wonderful organization of volunteers west of the Potomac, plastic under McClellan's skillful hand, in the full bloom of its evolution. Cushing entered into the spirit of soldier-making and of earthwork construction, and his labors were of acknowledged value. But what McClellan was competent to do was soon done. The great review at Bailey's Cross Roads was a source of astonishment to the expert spectators from other nations who observed the accuracy of its military movements and the excellent bearing of the 70,000 men who might easily have marched to Centerville the next day and squelched the Virginia section of the rebellion with not a hundredth part of the effort that was required for that purpose in the years following. It must have been with a heavy heart that Alonzo Cushing, always longing for effective action, saw the splendid opportunities of the winter of 1861 squandered in useless delays.

Although he made no complaint, the experience of Howard during 1861 afforded ground for greater personal vexation. He had raised a company from among the newspaper men of Chicago. They had elected him captain, but for some reason their services were not accepted by the Illinois state authorities, and he reluctantly resumed his regular work, pursuing it until he could no longer resist the call of his country to the field. He therefore enlisted (March 24, 1862) as a private soldier in Battery B, First Illinois Artillery, in which he afterwards served faithfully and with as much credit as a private is usually thought entitled to, through several strenuous campaigns, including the operations about Vicksburg. There can be no reasonable doubt that his services as a private would furnish material for a story of interest and instruction; but no record of them is attainable, and the outline of his military life must here be postponed until after the earlier notable achievements of his younger brothers shall have been narrated.

With William, events were shaping themselves as he desired, except that the fighting was not quite as plentiful as he wished. On November 22, 1861, eighteen days after his eighteenth birthday anniversary, he wrote to his cousin Mary (at East Troy, Wisconsin, then recently married to Mr. C. W. Smith), from the "Cambridge," a lively account of an expedition into the Rappahannock River to cut out a vessel loaded with wheat, which was burned on being found hard and fast on shore. Returning, the boat was bombarded by cannon and musketry along the river bank. Of the concluding scenes of this expedition, he gives the following account:

The Southerners had stationed a company of their riflemen in a house, and watching them I fired canister till I had for the time silenced their great gun. I then threw a thirty-pound shell which burst directly in the house, tearing it in pieces, and as I afterwards learned, killing and wounding some twenty-five men. This dis-heartened the rebels, and a few more rounds from the gun and the rifles finished the work, and we quietly steamed down the river to the ship. * * * Of course I was glad to learn that I had been mentioned with credit in the official dispatch to the Navy department.

There was nothing else that winter in the way of adventure of his own that he thought worth mention; but he was a spectator (March 9, 1862), of the battle in Hampton Roads between the "Monitor" and the "Merrimac," wherein the destiny of wooden ships was settled for all time.

Alonzo was prone, with the anonymous poet, to,

Count that day lost whose low-descending sunSaw at his hands no worthy action done.

The test of worthiness with him was usefulness to the Union cause. So when the defenses of the capital were completed, he took up the duties (January 21, 1862) of ordnance officer for the Second Corps, at General Sumner's headquarters—until the return, in March, of the Army of the Potomac from its fruitless promenade to Centerville, and to the vacant quarters of the Confederate army there. On March 21 he was commanded to act as an aid-de-camp to Sumner, in charge of topographical work, which was considered particularly important in the operations at Yorktown. This lasted from April 5 to May 4, when it was again discovered that the Confederates had declined to wait for the annihilation prepared for them if they would delay moving until McClellan should get all his parallels in shape according to Vauban, or whomever the authority on earthworks then in vogue may have been.

The last year of Alonzo's Life

In the "seven days" before Richmond, his conduct was such as to receive very high praise from Sumner. Before the end of July, an order of transfer was made for him to become an officer of the Topographical Engineers, the most intellectually elevated of all the branches of the army.

To foregather with the military high-brows was not an aspiration of this soldier, however, and he respectfully declined the honor. Notwithstanding his preference for artillery work, McClellan ordered him to perform the duties of assistant topographical engineer at his own headquarters when he set out on the Maryland campaign, and kept him at the work as long as he himself was in command of the Army of the Potomac. The general had a keen eye for unusual merit in young soldiers; one of the causes of the personal affection felt towards him by the great bulk of his officers and men was his promptness to acknowledge their merits.

On November 5, McClellan was superseded by General Burnside, and the Army of the Potomac was soon after re-organized by separation into three "grand divisions" under the respective commands of Generals Sumner, Franklin, and Hooker, for the right, the left, and the centre.

The right grand division was naturally to take the initiative in future movements, and Sumner wanted Cushing for topographical work at his headquarters. The required surveying and map-making were not objectionable to the young man, so long as no active operations were in sight, and his labors in this direction also received warm commendation from the commanding officers. Indeed, no task was ever placed upon the shoulders of Alonzo Hersford Cushing, whether in civil or in military life, so far as I have been able to ascertain, that was not well and cheerfully done.

Facsimile of part of letter from Alonzo H. Cushing to his brother Milton; written after the fights before Richmond in 1862. For group photograph alluded to in postscript, see frontispiece to this volume.

The disastrous battle of Fredericksburg occurred on December 13, and Lieutenant Cushing cut loose for the day from grand division headquarters, taking position by the side of General Couch, commanding the Second Corps, with whom he found ample opportunity for deeds of heroic daring, which were acknowledged in a general way in Couch's report of the part taken by his corps in the fight. "Lieutenant Cushing," he says, "was with me throughout the battle, and acted with his well-known gallantry." Such further representation of Cushing's conduct was made to the War Department that President Lincoln brevetted him captain, to date from the 13th of December, "for gallant and meritorious services at the battle of Fredericksburg, Va." A leave of absence for a three weeks' visit home was also accorded to him from January 26, 1863—his last opportunity for a glimpse of life among his relatives and friends. On returning to Virginia, Cushing resumed command of his battery, and never afterwards left it until his glorious death on the third day at Gettysburg.

The battle of Chancellorsville was prefaced by several tentative actions, beginning at Fitzhugh's Crossing on the Rappahannock, below Fredericksburg (April 29, 1863), and continuing at Spottsylvania Court House, Fredericksburg, Salem Heights and Marye's Heights before culminating in "The Wilderness" on May 3.

What Cushing did in this fighting, I have not been able to ascertain; but that it partook of the character of his service is evident because the President gave him the brevet of major, dating from May 2, 1863, "for gallant and meritorious services at the battle of Chancellorsville." It may incidentally be mentioned that in those days a presidential brevet was of more importance than it afterwards became under subsequent acts of Congress. Originally it entitled the officer, if he pleased, to wear the uniform of his brevet rank, to be addressed by his brevet title, and to serve as of his brevet rank when specially detailed. Under later laws he could not properly wear the uniform of rank above that which belonged to him by regular commission.

It was a short two months from Chancellorsville to Gettysburg, and the concluding two weeks were full of incident for the men engaged, though history has not considered it worth while to note the incidents in any length of detail. Even the *Rebellion Records* published by the national government have little to say of the marches of the two great opposing armies from the Rappahannock to the sources of the Monocacy and beyond.

But the destiny of the Republic was entwined in the serpentine paths of Lee's army going down the west side of the Blue Ridge, and Hooker's on the east side, both headed towards the north. A change of commanders of the Army of the Potomac was also impending, of which the soldiers knew nothing, but which was all the time a puzzle and worry to the corps and division leaders.

Cushing, with an ever cheerful face, was found with his battery in front of each successive mountain pass reached by the advance of Lee's forces, as the latter moved along the valley of the Shenandoah on the western side of the range.

On June 25, Hancock concentrated the Second Corps, of which he was now the head, at Haymarket, only a few miles from Manassas and Thoroughfare Gaps. There the Confederate cavalry general, Stuart, was surprised to find so large a force and went back over the mountains—again northward, in the track of Lee, instead of delaying the Union army by a raid on its rear, as he had expected to do when he was detached from the main Confederate army before crossing the Potomac.

That Hancock should parallel Stuart's march was a matter of course, and on June 30 he was in bivouac at Taneytown, half a dozen miles south of Gettysburg. The next day the curtain was partially withdrawn from the most magnificent spectacle of a conflict of ideas, supported by fighting men, that the Western Continent, at least, ever witnessed. Hancock's corps, to which Cushing was attached, was resting at Taneytown all day; but after the death of General Reynolds, Hancock was on the battlefield north of the town; and although the battery was with the rest of the corps, there can be little doubt that Cushing was with him personally as a temporary aide. My reason for assuming this is, that the brevet of lieutenant-colonel, made out for him the next day, stated that the honor was conferred "for conspicuous gallantry at the battle of Gettysburg, Pa., July 1, 1863."

I wish that I had even one letter written by Lieutenant Cushing between Chancellorsville and Gettysburg, but I have knowledge of none. Such a document would admit us to his inner feelings. From his acts alone, and from what his most intimate acquaintances in the army have written, our judgment must be formed. A history of the great battle can not be given here; but fortunately no account of the engagement by a reputable writer fails to take notice of the part taken by the brave young son of Wisconsin in stemming the high tide of rebellion on the third day of the conflict. In Colonel Haskell's absorbing story, a tribute is also paid to Cushing's endeavors on the second day.[6] To that narrative the reader is referred for that, among other living pictures of the deadly struggle.

[6] Frank Aretas Haskell, *The Battle of Gettysburg* (Wisconsin History Commission: Reprints, No. 1, November, 1908), pp. 102, 116, 120, 121.

For me, it must be sufficient to portray as well as I can the final stand of Battery A and its commander at the focus of the last day's fighting. Our line of battle stretched along the ridge overlooking the valley between it and the southern armies; along its whole length, fighting was either imminent or actually in evidence. The thunder of artillery was like a continuous roar that filled the atmosphere. The fire of most of the one hundred and fifteen Confederate cannon then in action seemed to be directed by a kind of instinct towards the point in our line where the batteries of Cushing, Woodruff, and Rorty were belching destruction in the faces of their assailants, a mile and a half away. The artillery practice of the Southerners was good. Between the afternoon hours of 1 and 3, many of our artillery organizations suffered severe losses by the bursting of ammunition chests, the breaking of wheels of gun carriages, and the overthrow of horses that lay in death struggles on the ground. Men were hit, also. Among the first to receive a serious wound that fateful afternoon was Cushing himself. Both thighs were torn open by a fragment of shell—under which ill fortune, said General Webb in his report, "he fought for an hour and a half, cool, brave, competent."

The commander of his brigade, Colonel Hall, reported that:

he challenged the admiration of all who saw him. Three of his limbers were blown up and changed with the caisson limbers, under fire. Several wheels were shot off his guns and replaced, till at last, severely wounded himself, his officers all killed or wounded, and with but cannoneers enough to man a section, he pushed his gun to the fence in front and was killed while serving his last canister into the ranks of the advancing enemy.

Hall's last reference is to a later hour of July 3 than that to which I at present wish to call attention. It is near 3 o'clock in the afternoon. To give them an opportunity to cool off somewhat, our eighty cannon have been ordered to cease firing. The artillerymen throw themselves on the ground to rest, or help clear away dead horses and other debris from about the guns. Our infantry line is closely fronted by stone walls and other fences along the Emmetsburg road, or a short distance back from that thoroughfare. The protection thus afforded is not at all certain, even when sods are packed against the fences, for a solid cannon shot or fragment of shell may penetrate such an earthwork, when reinforced only by a wooden fence, as though it were a row of cigar boxes. It affords some defense, however, against bullets which strike diagonally, or are fired over a considerable distance. Down in front of the hill called "Round Top," Kilpatrick's cavalry are worrying the right of the enemy; but that fails to disturb those in the neighborhood of Cushing, who was almost in the middle of the outstretched line of Union troops.

Now Pickett's splendid column of 17,000 Virginians emerge from the woods on the farther side of the valley, and direct their course towards the point where Cushing is holding a front place. Other Union batteries are hurling solid shot at the enemy, as they start on their fatal journey across the valley. Confederate cannon send volleys of shell over the heads of their infantry, into the groups of our cannoneers, who continue to pelt the advancing column. The iron shells burst in midair, with puffs of smoke, like sporadic ejections from the smoke-pipe of a locomotive engine, but with resounding clangs. If the puff from a bursting shell is behind you, or directly overhead, you are safe from the effects of that explosion; but if seen in front, the iron fragments are likely to cut through the flesh and bones of some of you; for the forward motion of the shell is not lost by its explosion, although the pieces acquire additional directions of flight. There is a composite of demoniac noises, every missile splitting the atmosphere with its own individual hum, whir, or shriek; the musketry rattle like hail, and the deep boom of cannonry lends its all-pervading basso to the symphony of thousands of instruments and voices.

As the grim column hurries on, our batteries change from solid shot to shell, tearing great gaps in the advancing lines; but these resolutely close up, and move forward to attain a distance from which their rifled muskets shall be used effectively against us. This reached, they begin blazing away. Cushing and his neighbors open upon them with canister and case, every discharge sending a shower of small metal into the approaching ranks. However, the survivors press onward, firing as they come, and the batteries behind them send their shell among our cannon, killing horses and men, and overthrowing guns, but not yet harming afresh the young hero whom we are particularly noting. Woodruff and Rorty are slain, though, at the head of other batteries close at hand.

At last a bullet pierces Cushing's shoulder. He simply laughs at the hurt, calling to Webb, his division commander, "I'll give them one more shot. Good-by!" As he serves the last round of canister, another bullet strikes him in the mouth, passing through the base of his brain, and he falls forward, bereft of life, into the arms of his clarion-voiced, resolute, and fearless orderly sergeant, Frederick Fuger, whom he has called to his side to convey his orders to the men.

The Union line of infantry was also making use of its muskets, in trying to stop the Confederate assault. The aim of the soldiers was more or less accurate in proportion to the nerve-control exercised by the respective individuals engaged. For not all of the forces attacking or attacked are fully conscious of what they are doing, when the surrounding air is pregnant with death. Some try to shoot with their eyes shut, and others forget to place a percussion cap on their firearm. Out of over thirty-seven thousand muskets left on the Gettysburg battle-ground by soldiers of both sides, no longer able to carry them, nearly a third were loaded with more than one cartridge each, and many with more than two. We pardon the confusion of mind exhibited before his audience, by a young actor or speaker, and it surely is no less to be expected that unaccustomed soldiers should often feel trepidation when face to face with death.

Despite the firing from our side, a hundred of Armistead's men kept close to their chief, leaping the fence next to Cushing's battery, just behind him, and in time to see their leader lay hand on Cushing's last cannon and fall dying with a bullet through his body—only a few yards from where his late indomitable opponent lay dead.

By the side of that field-piece, went out the lives of two as gallant warriors as ever wielded sword on battlefield, and Cushing still lacked six months of completing his twenty-third year of life. The Southern soldiers who thought they had taken the battery, now rushed back or surrendered on the spot, and the flood tide of rebellion began to recede, never again to attain so dangerous a height, although often rising somewhat uncomfortably.

The loss of a son so high in aspiration and so capable for the achievement of necessary tasks, must have been a grievous stroke for his mother to bear— she who had placed her greatest reliance upon him, rather than upon his brothers. For her compensation for such a loss, she was allowed a pension of seventeen dollars per month until the year of her death (which happened March 26, 1891), when the allowance was increased to fifty dollars. In this case the national government was certainly very much the reverse of liberal in its recognition of the services of a noble mother, who had formed the character of a noble son whose life was joyfully laid upon the altar of his country.

It is pleasant to be able to state that Sergeant Fuger, who took command of the battery after the death and disablement of its three commissioned officers taking part in the battle, was promoted to a lieutenancy in the regiment. He served in the regular order of grades until retired (about 1900) on account of age, as colonel, since which he has lived in the city of Washington. From a letter recently written by him to Mrs. Bouton, I am permitted to make the following transcript:

In answer to your letter received yesterday morning, I would say that the best friend I had was your dear brother, Alonzo H. Cushing, First Lieutenant 4th Artillery, commanding Battery A, 4th Artillery, at the battle of Gettysburg. On the morning of July 4, 1863, I received an order from Gen. Hancock, commanding 2d Corps, to send your brother's body to West Point for burial. I placed the body in care of two non-commissioned officers who were slightly wounded, to take it to West Point.

The manner of your brother's death was this: When the enemy was within about four hundred yards, Battery A opened with single charges of canister. At that time Cushing was wounded in the right shoulder, and within a few seconds after that he was wounded in the abdomen; a very severe and painful wound. He called and told me to stand by him so that I could impart his orders to the battery. He became very ill and suffered frightfully. I wanted him to go to the rear. "No," he said, "I stay right here and fight it out, or die in the attempt."

When the enemy got within two hundred yards, double and triple charges of canister were used. Those charges opened immense gaps in the Confederate lines. Lieut. Milne, who commanded the right half-battery, was killed when the enemy was within two hundred yards of the battery. When the enemy came within about one hundred yards, Lieutenant Cushing was shot through the mouth and instantly killed. When I saw him fall forward, I caught him in my arms, ordered two men to take his body to the rear, and shouted to my men, as I was left in command, to fire triple charges of canister.

Owing to dense smoke, I could not see very far to the front, but to my utter astonishment I saw the Confederate General Armistead leap over the stone fence with quite a number of his men, landing right in the midst of our battery, but my devoted cannoneers and drivers stood their ground, fighting hand to hand with pistols, sabers, handspikes and rammers, and with the assistance of the Philadelphia brigade, the enemy collapsed and Pickett's charge was defeated. The gall and behavior of the men in Battery A was entirely due to your brother's training and example set on numerous battlefields.

Lieutenant Cushing, my commander, was a most able soldier, of excellent judgment and great decision of character. Devoted to his profession, he was most faithful in the discharge of every duty, accurate and thorough in its performance. Possessed of mental and physical vigor, joined to the kindest of hearts, he commanded the love and respect of all who knew him. His superiors placed implicit confidence in him, as well they might. His fearlessness and resolution displayed in many actions were unsurpassed, and his noble death at Gettysburg should present an example for emulation to patriotic defenders of the country through all time to come.

General Armistead fell, mortally wounded, where I stood, about seven yards from where Lieutenant Cushing, his young and gallant adversary, was killed. In height your brother was five feet nine inches, in weight about one hundred and fifty pounds, good long limbs, broad shoulders, blue eyes, dark brown hair, smooth face, without beard or mustache, and rather swarthy complexion.

From other communications of the colonel, addressed to myself, I learn that Lieutenant Cushing personally saved the battery from capture at the battle of Antietam; that its loss at Gettysburg was two officers killed and one wounded, seven enlisted men killed and thirty-eight wounded, and eighty-three horses killed out of ninety taken into the action. Not an uninjured wheel remained, and nine ammunition chests were blown up. Ninety enlisted men belonging to the battery were on duty at the beginning of the fight.

Corporal Thomas Moon has also written his recollections of the day, and although his memory seems somewhat at fault in relation to certain matters, his description is worth reading. He says:

Cushing was a small-sized man with blue eyes, smooth face and auburn hair, and looked more like a school girl than a warrior; but he was the best fighting man I ever saw. Our battery arrived on the field July 2 and took position on the left of the 2d corps. I was sent to the rear with the 4th caisson. We went back over the hill close to General Meade's headquarters. When the heavy cannonading commenced on the 3d we went further to the rear. About the time that Pickett was ordered to charge, I was ordered to the battery. I was informed by the courier that I would find the battery on the right of the 2d corps, at the grove and angle. My horse made a good run for about a mile. I found my piece, the 4th, still on her wheels, and all the canister we had piled up around her. I had been on the ground but a few minutes before I found the gun hot and firing slow. A very few minutes passed until the smoke raised, and we saw the head of Pickett's column within three hundred yards of us. We had the opportunity of our lives; just what an artilleryman wants. We had a flank fire on them and enough canister to stop them, but before they got to the stone wall in front we were out of ammunition and my gun was dismounted. Lieutenant Cushing was on the right. We both got to the piece in front about the same time. I found the piece out of canister, started back to the limber, looked back and saw General Armistead with his hat on his sword yelling to his men, and Cushing being held up by some infantry officer. If I had stayed at the gun as long as Cushing did, I would have been there yet. Our guns were all disabled, limbers and caissons blown up, men and horses killed and wounded, and the battery under command of a First Sergeant (afterwards lieutenant) Frederick Fuger, a 10-year man, and as fine a soldier and officer as ever faced an enemy. I was on duty that night—had three men under me. All we had to guard was a few dead men. We took Lieutenant Cushing and three or four men off the field. It rained all night.

HOWARD B. CUSHING

Now, as to Cushing's wounds. One piece of shell struck him in the thighs; another piece struck him in the shoulder; but he stuck to the guns until a ball struck him right under the nose. He fell on one side of the piece and General Armistead on the other. His right thumb was burned to the bone, serving vent without a thumb-pad. We were all tired, powder-burned and bruised; so we laid the dead men together and lay atop of them all night. The next morning we took Cushing's fatigue blouse off, and his cook got that after I took off the shoulder-straps. I carried them till the next winter, and gave them to his brother (Howard) at Brandy Station.

Later Naval Service of William Cushing

Up to the day of Alonzo Cushing's death, the reputation of his younger brother William kept pretty even pace with his own. William's judgment in moments of imminent peril seemed to be unerring, so that a venture with him appeared to his companions to have but one chance of failure—the death of the adventurer himself. But this had been challenged with so many styles of defiance, as to cause the more superstitious among the sailors to believe him invulnerable. They were always ready and anxious to accompany him on those of his expeditions that appeared the most desperate. The unlimited devotion of his men and under-officers is one of the most valuable assets of a military or naval officer. This, with his other qualities, procured for him a commission as lieutenant on July 16, 1862, nearly four months before he attained the age of twenty years.

William was thereupon given the position of second officer on the gunboat "Perry," on the North Carolina coast, at an age when a midshipman or master's mate, or even a lieutenant, is usually content to play a very subordinate part in warfare.

Soon after this (September following), his superior officer, Lieutenant-Commander Flusser, was ordered up the Blackwater River with his own and two other boats to co-operate with a land force in preventing the escape of about seven thousand Confederates stationed at Franklin, with Norfolk as their ultimate object. The naval contingent was at the rendezvous at the agreed time; that from the army failed to make connection. It was an unpleasant predicament for the boats, but they fought their way back, down the narrow channel of the river, the banks of which for many miles were lined with infantry and artillery.

At one point, when the decks were being swept by the enemy's bullets, and a boarding party was making a dash for the "Perry," Cushing called a half dozen of his men to help him get a howitzer into position, to meet the boarders with canister. When his volunteers were all killed or disabled, he took the gun alone and trained it upon the assailants with such effect that they ran away. In Flusser's report of the affair he took occasion to say:

I desire to mention as worthy of praise for great gallantry, Lieutenant W. B. Cushing, who ran the field-piece out amid a storm of bullets, took a sure and deliberate aim at the rebels and sent a charge of canister among them that completely silenced their fire at that point.

On October 26, 1862, Admiral S. P. Lee reports:

Lieutenant W. B. Cushing has been put in command of the gunboat Ellis, and is increasing his reputation by active operations.

On October 18, William had written to his cousin:

I am alone, inside the outer bar. The nearest friendly vessel or citizen is forty miles away. Three miles off, up the inlet, is the rebel town of Swansboro. I am going to run up and take possession in a few days, when I have burned up enough coal to lighten my vessel so I can cross the other bar. * * * You see I have a sort of roving commission and can run around to suit myself. * * * If under these circumstances I can not stir the rebels up in more places than one, it will be strange indeed.

He ran up to Swansboro in due time and burned the "Adelaide" with a $100,000 cargo, besides destroying salt works. On November 23, he worked his vessel to Jacksonville, a depot for blockade runners, and on the way caused a ship loaded with turpentine to be burned. At the town he captured a lot of guns and other public property, and started back. About 5 o'clock p. m. he found and shelled a camp of Confederate troops on the river bank, and came to anchor at nightfall, staying all night with his prizes, two large schooners.

The next morning Cushing moved on. Reaching a difficult passage in the river, he was attacked by shore artillery, but replied so vigorously that the gunners on shore were driven away, and he passed along. Shortly after, however, the "Ellis" ran aground and had to be burned, but not before her outfit had been mostly removed to one of the schooners, amid some hours of fighting. Then Cushing and his companions escaped in a small boat to the schooner which, with its companion, was taken back to open water.

He asked for a court of inquiry on account of the loss of his gunboat, but the admiral said there was no need, and the Navy Department at Washington approved, saying, "We don't care for the loss of a vessel when fought so gallantly as that."

A much thicker volume than this would be required to tell the stories of the young sailor's various adventures during the ensuing year. The reader must be content with relations of occasional adventures, sometimes in Cushing's own language. Our hero was now given command of the "Commodore Barney," a steamer of five hundred and thirteen tons with a very powerful battery, and, according to his own statement, a good crew of over one hundred men and thirteen officers. He continues, in his letter (written April 5) to his cousin, Mrs. Smith, at East Troy: "Of course I am as proud as a peacock at being the only lieutenant in the regular navy who has a [separate] command."

William's Letter to His Mother

On the 15th he writes his mother a letter which is given here nearly in full, for it indicates better than almost anything else some of the prominent traits of his character as developed at that time, when boyish impulses were mixed with striking elements of manliness. He talks with the intimate frankness of a son who is still in love with his mother and wishes her to share in his triumph:

Another fight and another victory! Again I have passed through the ordeal of fire and blood, and again I thank God for being safe in life and limb. Suffolk is besieged by the enemy, thirty thousand strong, and contains an army of fifteen thousand to defend it. The town is situated on this river (the Nansemond) and its water communication must remain open or our force will be in a desperate position. Who do you suppose was selected to perform the dangerous task of guarding the rear, and preventing the crossing of ten thousand of the flower of the southern army? Who but your son, that ex-midshipman, ex-master's mate, hair-brained, scapegrace, Will Cushing! Yes, it is even so. I am senior officer commanding in the Nansemond river. I have my vessel and two others now. I had two more, but they were disabled in action, and have been towed to Hampton Roads. I am six miles from the city, at a place called Western Branch, the point most desired by the enemy. I draw too much water to go up further, but sent my light boats up above.

Yesterday morning, as they were on their way down, they encountered a battery at a distance of three hundred yards, and swarms of riflemen in the bushes on the banks. A sharp action ensued, in which two of the boats were disabled, and but one left uninjured, but the captain of her, like a brave fellow as he is, got them around the point out of range, and we managed to get them as far as the bar here when one, the Mount Washington, got aground. The rebels soon appeared in force, bent upon driving us and crossing the river. They opened with artillery from two positions a cross-fire, and their seven pieces sent a hail of shot and shell around us.

I had but two vessels afloat, but I silenced their fire in an hour. In a short time they again went into action; this time unmasking a regularly constructed battery not five hundred yards from us, and so situated as to rake the narrow channel completely. It was impossible to get our disabled steamer off from the bar until high water, five hours ahead, and I determined to fight on the spot as long as the Barney [his own vessel] was above the water. I sent the light steamer down to guard another coveted point, and was soon exchanging death calls with the enemy.

Well, it was a hard fight and at close quarters most of the time; so close that their infantry riddled the two vessels with bullets. Crash! go the bulkheads; a rifle shell was exploded on our deck, tearing flesh and woodwork. A crash like thunder is our reply—and our heavy shell makes music in the air, and explodes among our traitor neighbors with a dull, sullen roar of defiance. Up goes the battle-flag and at once the air is filled with the smoke of furious battle, and the ear thrills with the unceasing shriek and whistle of all the shell and rifled bolts that sinful man has devised to murder his fellow creatures. Crash! Crash! Splinters are flying in the air; great pools of blood are on the deck, and the first cry of wounded men in agony rises on the soft spring air. The dead can not speak, but there they lie motionless, lifeless and mangled, who a moment ago smiled on the old flag that floated over them, and fought for its glory and honor. Sprinkle ashes over the slippery deck; the work must still go on. The rifled gun—my best—is disabled, for three shots have struck it; the muzzle is gone, the elevator is carried away and the carriage is broken.

Steady, men, steady; fill up the places of the killed and wounded. Don't throw a shot away. The wheel of the howitzer is torn off by the shell and the gun rendered useless. Never mind; work the remaining guns with a will, for we can and must be victorious. And so the time wore away until the rising river promised to release the imprisoned steamer, when I signaled to the light steamer to move up and take her in tow. This duty was gallantly performed, and the old Barney remained alone under the rebel cannon. * * *

My vessel is riddled with cannon balls and bullets, and I have lost three killed and nine wounded—four of them mortally—men who lost legs and arms. The loss on the other vessels is proportionally severe. I am no braggart, but I challenge the world to furnish a more determined fight, or a victory more richly earned. The enemy shall not cross here. I will not give way an inch. Even now the thickets on the banks are alive with their sharpshooters, and as I write, the quick whirr of the rifle bullet is often heard, sent from the bank five hundred yards ahead in the vain hope of injuring the hated Yankee. A good providence seems to watch over my fortunes, tho' I do not deserve its protection. I may go into action again at any moment, probably tomorrow. I have every confidence in my gallant crew and officers and do not doubt the result if my life is spared. Love to all.

In haste, Your affectionate son,

WILL.

After Gettysburg

When General Lee crossed the Potomac on his way to Gettysburg, William was called to Washington to be ready for action in defense of the capital, should it need defense. Hearing of his brother's death on the night of its occurrence, he obtained permission and left for the battlefield, intending to ask the privilege of handling Alonzo's guns, which undoubtedly he was perfectly capable of doing. Those guns were out of the business, however, and he had to satisfy himself with looking through the field, of which he said long afterwards, "My mind fails to bring up any picture that is so grand, or solemn, or so mournful as that great theater of death."

A month afterwards, William was in command of the "Shoboken," a former ferry boat made over into a vessel well-adapted to the shallow waters of the Carolina coasts. With her he destroyed the blockade runner "Hebe," after a fight with a land battery.

A few nights later he took a crew of six men in a dingey, to a point on the beach four miles from the mouth of the inlet which was separated from the waters outside by a long and very narrow stretch of sandbank. Here he and his men carried the boat across the neck of land, and proceeded with it up the inlet to the anchorage of another blockade runner, where he took ten prisoners, burned the vessel and some valuable salt works, threw the shore armament into the water, and returned by the same route, regaining the "Shoboken" without loss of any kind.

The next day, William rejoined the squadron outside, which was engaged with a shore battery. Landing with twenty men, he captured the battery and took two rifled cannon back with him to the squadron.

The Destruction of the "Albemarle"

As it is impossible to crowd into this sketch any considerable proportion of the adventures of Lieutenant Cushing, it seems best in illustration of the extraordinary quality of his bravery, to proceed at once to the narrative of his famous exploit in the destruction of the Confederate ironclad "Albemarle," which earned for him further promotion, the engrossed thanks of Congress, and congratulatory addresses from civic bodies in every part of the North.

This ironclad was built on the lines of the old "Merrimac," and like the latter had met the fire of our biggest guns without injury. In April, 1864, she had attacked and recaptured the town of Plymouth, situated near the head of Albemarle Sound, eight miles above the place where the Sound receives the waters of Roanoke River. She had beaten off our fleet at that place, sunk its principal boat, the "Southfield," and killed the commander, Flusser, of whom we have spoken in connection with an earlier conflict. In May, the "Albemarle" steamed out into the Sound and simultaneously engaged seven of our vessels, destroying the "Sassacuse," which had unsuccessfully tried to overwhelm her by ramming beneath the water-line. The Union ironclads were not light enough to cross the bar in front of the entrance to the Sound, and the officers of our fleet were much puzzled as to how to be rid of the annoyance.

Cushing finally submitted two plans to Admiral Lee, either of which had, he thought, a fair chance of success. One was for him to take a hundred men, with India-rubber boats ready for inflation, lead them through the dense thickets of the swamps adjoining Plymouth, and after inflating the boats turn the sailors into a boarding party that should overpower the "Albemarle's" crew. The other was the one adopted, although with many misgivings on the part of the admiral and of the assistant secretary of the navy, Mr. Fox. It looked like a modern repetition of the dramatic episode of David and

Goliath, and they permitted themselves to hope that this youth of twenty-one might have as good fortune as his Biblical predecessor. In brief, it was arranged that William should proceed to New York and select two very small, low-pressure steamers, each carrying a howitzer and a torpedo. These he was secretly to convey along the coast to the Sound and there attack the big ironclad by night, in such manner as might appear best when the time was ripe for action.

The boats were secured. Each was about thirty feet long and carried a 12-pound howitzer, with a torpedo fastened to the end of a boom at the bow, the boom being fourteen feet long and supplied with a "goose-neck" hinge where it rested on the bow. One of the boats was lost before reaching Norfolk; but with the other Cushing went through the Chesapeake and Albemarle Canal to the Sound.

Starting at midnight, he found the Union fleet fifty miles up the Sound, expecting a visit from the enemy's ironclad. Here he explained the daring plan to his officers and men, and told them they were at liberty to go with him or not, as they might choose. All wished to go, and a few from other vessels also volunteered. On the night of October 27, the party steamed up the river.

What happened thereafter, is told so tersely by Cushing himself, in his formal report to Admiral Porter, that it seems fair to use his own words. Under date of October 30, he writes:

Sir: I have the honor to report that the rebel ironclad Albemarle is at the bottom of the Roanoke river.

On the night of the 27th, having prepared my steam launch, I proceeded up towards Plymouth with thirteen officers and men, partly volunteers from the squadron. The distance from the mouth of the river to the ram is about eight miles, the stream averaging in width some two hundred yards, and lined with the enemy's pickets.

A mile below the town was the wreck of the Southfield, surrounded by some schooners, and it was understood that a gun was mounted there to command the bend. I therefore took one of the Shamrock's cutters in tow, with orders to cast off and board at that point if we were hailed.

Our boat succeeded in passing the pickets, and even the Southfield within twenty yards without discovery, and we were not hailed until by the lookouts on the ram. The cutter was cast off and ordered below, however, while we made for our enemy under a full head of steam.

The rebels sprang their rattles, rang the bell and commenced firing, at the same time repeating their hail and seeming much confused. The light of a fire ashore showed me the ironclad, made fast to the wharf, with a pen of logs around her, about 30 feet from her side. Passing her closely, we made a complete circle so as to strike her fairly, and went into her, bows on.

By this time the enemy's fire was very severe, but a dose of canister at short range served to moderate their zeal and disturb their aim. Paymaster Swan of the Otsego was wounded near me, but how many more I know not. Three bullets struck my clothing and the air seemed full of them. In a moment we had struck the logs, just abreast the quarter port, breasting them in some feet, and our bows resting on them. The torpedo boom was then lowered, and by a vigorous pull I succeeded in driving the torpedo under the overhang, and exploded it at the same time that the Albemarle's gun was fired. A shot seemed to go crashing through my boat, and a dense mass of water rushed in from the torpedo, filling the launch and completely disabling her. The enemy then continued his fire at fifteen feet range, and demanded our surrender which I twice refused, ordering the men to save themselves, and removing my own coat and shoes. Springing into the river, I swam with others into the middle of the stream, the rebels failing to hit us. The most of our party were captured, some drowned, and only one escaped besides myself, and he in a different direction.

Acting Master's Mate Woodman, of the Commodore Hull, I met in the water half a mile below the town and assisted him as best I could, but failed to get him ashore. Completely exhausted, I managed to reach the shore, but was too weak to crawl out of the water until just at daylight, when I managed to creep into the swamp, close to the fort. While hiding a few feet from the path two of the Albemarle's officers passed, and I judged from their conversation that the ship was destroyed.

Some hours traveling in the swamp served to bring me out well below the town, when I sent a negro in to gain information, and found the ram was truly sunk. Proceeding through another swamp, I came to a creek and captured a skiff belonging to a picket of the enemy, and with this by 11 o'clock the next night made my way out to the Valley City. Acting Master's Mate William Howarth of the Monticello showed as usual conspicuous bravery. He is the same officer who has been with me twice in Wilmington harbor. I trust he may be promoted when exchanged, as well as Acting Third Assistant Engineer Stotesbury, who, being for the first time under fire, handled his engine promptly and with coolness. All the officers and men behaved in the most gallant manner. I will furnish their names to the Department as soon as they can be procured.

The cutter of the Shamrock boarded the Southfield, but found no gun. Four prisoners were taken there. The ram is now completely submerged, and the enemy has sunk three schooners in the river to obstruct the passage of our ships. I desire to call the attention of the admiral and the Department to the spirit manifested by the sailors on the ships in these sounds. But few men were wanted, but all hands were eager to go into the action, many offering their chosen shipmates a month's pay to resign in their favor.

I am, sir, very respectfully your obedient servant,

W. B. CUSHING,

Lieutenant United States Navy.

So much by way of requisite and necessary formality from an inferior officer who does something, to a superior who has the right to know all about what the other has been doing. Still, the young man who has not yet attained the maturity of twenty-two years discloses the ability on his part to say clearly and concisely what conveys his meaning, although not always in strict conformity with rhetorical rules. Of course he does not present himself as a candidate for honors in a class in rhetoric; but he does possess the essential of success in that direction also, if he cares for it. The language that is for use, rather than for ornament, is the language of lasting character.

But from motives of modesty and discipline combined, the lieutenant did not tell his superiors in office all the items of fact that other people would like to know. Matters of interest omitted in the formal report, are noted in many cases in Cushing's private journal, and that document was handed over to Mrs. Harriet Prescott Spofford for use in an extended magazine article.[7] From that and other sources I will add somewhat to the story told officially to the admiral.

[7] *Harper's Monthly*, June, 1874.

Cushing had a way of rapidly and judiciously thinking for himself. On approaching near enough to the "Albemarle" to make out her presence, he concluded to board her and take her down the river to the Union lines, trusting to the confusion of a night surprise to help the daring scheme to a successful issue. His view was correct; but just as he was about to put it into execution a challenge rang out from the ironclad, followed by the rattle of musketry from the guards who stood at their stations. Luckily for the assailants, the flame of a bonfire of pine knots and other light-wood flared upward, and Cushing saw what without it he would have been unable to see—a surrounding semicircular boom of logs, fastened end-to-end by iron links and hooks, making futile any attempt at boarding.

He was standing on the deck, in full view of the enemy, who were doing their best to kill him; but the whistling bullets could not disturb the quickness and accuracy of his judgment. In front of him lay two signal lines, one of which was attached to the engineer's ankle, and one to the arm of the officer in charge of the torpedo beam—besides other lines, one of which was arranged to push the torpedo under the vessel to be attacked, while still another was to explode the torpedo at the supreme moment. A mistake in relation to either of these would have been fatal to the undertaking.

But Cushing made no mistake. On being signaled, the engineer below backed the boat out into the stream, and then headed straight on to the middle of the line of logs, carrying the bow of the launch partly over, so that the torpedo when let down would be within reach of the ironclad. The officer in charge of the sweep was then signaled, and lowered the torpedo boom, which Cushing caused to be crowded under the "Albemarle's" side. Then he pulled a cord that released a suspended iron ball, which in its turn fell upon a percussion cap, thus exploding the infernal machine and blowing a hole through the side of the ram. To me, this perfection of action in the midst of death-dealing missiles, seems almost beyond the scope of mere human endeavor.

Plenty of men in both armies could, without flinching, march up to the mouths of cannon and into a storm of bullets; but under such circumstances as surrounded young Cushing when destroying the "Albemarle," such an exhibition of coolness absolutely imperturbable was neither seen nor imagined by me, in what I saw of the War. I doubt much if there ever was a parallel instance. Possibly the exploits of the elder brother, Alonzo, at Gettysburg, were as remarkable; but if so, they lacked a minute chronicler. With the latter, no complicated calculations nor deliberate weighing of comparative probabilities were apparently necessary to be employed, in order to accomplish what he wanted to do. Although among the bravest of the brave, it is not shown that Alonzo was in every respect as unquestionably the complete master in battle, of the lesser, equally with the greatest, of his mental faculties as was the case with his younger brother. William was as alert, resourceful, indefatigable as he might have been at a game of whist, or in the solution of a mathematical problem in the quietude of his chamber.

But escape from the Southern soldiery at Plymouth was purchased at the price of misery—and, ten years later, of a lamentable death. In a published paper by him, he refers to his experience in the river, after the explosion of the torpedo:[8]

[8] *Battles and Leaders of the Civil War* (N. Y., Century Co., 1884-88), vol. 4, p. 638.

I directed my course towards the town side of the river, not making much headway, as my strokes were now very feeble, my clothes being soaked and heavy, and little chop-seas splashing with a chocking persistence into my mouth every time that I gasped for breath. Still there was a determination not to sink, a will not to give up; and I kept up a sort of mechanical motion long after my bodily force was in fact expended. At last, and not a moment too soon, I touched the soft mud, and in the excitement of the first shock I half raised my body and made one step forward; then fell, and remained half in the mud and half in the water until daylight, unable even to crawl on hands and knees, nearly frozen, with brain in a whirl, but with one thing strong in me—the fixed determination to escape. The prospect of drowning, starvation, death in the swamps—all seemed less evils than that of surrender.

At twenty-two, one does not think of remote consequences, but human constitutions are not so made up as to remain uninjured by such violent usage. The commander of the "Albemarle," Captain A. F. Warley, contributed the following note to Cushing's paper, which should not be omitted here, in the interest of fairness:[9]

[9] Ibid, p. 642.

The crew of the Albemarle numbered but sixty, too small a force to allow me to keep an armed watch on deck at night and to do outside picketing besides. Moreover, to break the monotony of the life and keep down ague, I had always out an exhibition of ten men, who were uniformly successful in doing a fair amount of damage to the enemy. It was about 3 a. m. The night was dark and slightly rainy, and the launch was close to us when we hailed and the alarm was given—so close that the gun could not be depressed enough to reach her; so the crew were sent in the shield with muskets, and kept up a heavy fire on the launch as she slowly forced her way over the chain of logs and ranged by us within a few feet. As she reached the bow of the Albemarle I heard a report as of an unshotted gun, and a piece of wood fell at my feet. Calling the carpenter, I told him a torpedo had been exploded, and ordered him to examine and report to me, saying nothing to any one else. He soon reported "a hole in her bottom big enough to drive a wagon in." By this time I heard voices from the launch: "We surrender," etc., etc. I stopped our fire and sent out Mr. Long, who brought back all those who had been in the launch, except the gallant captain and three of her crew, all of whom took to the water. Having seen to their safety, I turned my attention to the Albemarle, and found her resting on bottom in eight feet of water, her upper works above water. That is the way the Albemarle was destroyed, and a more gallant thing was not done during the war.

A special message came from President Lincoln, recommending a vote of thanks by Congress, so that the young hero might be advanced to the grade of lieutenant-commander. This was immediately followed by the vote requested, and by his promotion to that rank, under the law providing "That any line officer of the Navy or Marine Corps may be advanced one grade, if upon recommendation of the President by name he receives the thanks of Congress for highly distinguished conduct in conflict with the enemy, or for extraordinary heroism in the lines of his profession." The importance, as well as the "highly distinguished" character, of the exploit with the "Albemarle" may be understood when it is learned that not only were the Carolina Sounds thereafter free to all such of our vessels as were of sufficiently light draft, but the town of Plymouth fell a few days later also, without a struggle. Even Cushing's coat, which he had cast off when he leaped from the launch into the river, was returned to him. The back of it was shot away, and there were other bullet holes through it; but a gold chain remained safely sewed under the collar, where he had caused it to be placed in honor of the girl to whom it belonged.

At Fort Fisher and Afterwards

After this promotion, Cushing took command of the admiral's flagship, the "Malvern," and in December was engaged in the operations at Fort Fisher, where in various attempts to capture that stronghold, so many failures had been recorded against both our army and navy. In an open skiff there, he performed a service as perilous as before, although less spectacular. This was the buoying the channel for the fleet, which task occupied him for about six hours under a shower of shot and shell from the fort.

On January 12, 1865, the bombardment was resumed from sixty vessels, and after three days of that exercise an assault was ordered, in which Lieutenant-Commander Cushing was permitted to take part. It proved to be one of the bloodiest little affrays of the war. Two of his classmates at Annapolis, Lieutenants B. H. Porter and S. W. Preston, were killed by his side; which caused him, he said, the bitterest tears he had ever shed. No other officer being near him, he rallied a few hundred men and was about to resume the assault, when he received orders to join the land forces under General Ames. He then had the satisfaction of witnessing the surrender of the fort before midnight.

After the works had been taken, Cushing proceeded to round up all the pilots in the vicinity, and by threatening to hang them procured all necessary information about the signals used for the guidance of the blockade runners who were in the habit of coming in at that point. Within four or five days, one of that class, the "Charlotte," commanded by a British ex-naval officer, steamed up to her anchorage, bringing two English army officers as well as a valuable cargo of arms and ammunition. Gratified at their successful trip, the officers were enjoying a banquet in honor of the event. Cushing, who liked surprises, stepped into the cabin and informed them that they were prisoners, but that he would join them in a glass of the champagne with which the table was loaded. The Englishmen made the best of the predicament, but the feast was interrupted by the announcement that another steamer, the "Stag," was coming up the river, whereupon their young captor excused himself to attend to the fresh arrival.

The war was now practically over, and during the few additional months of its continuance no further adventures appear to Cushing's credit. In 1867 he was given command of the "Maumee," and attached to the Pacific squadron, where life was no longer strenuous. On January 31, 1872, he was made full commander, and in July, 1873, placed in charge of the "Wyoming." In November of the same year he heard of the execution of several of the crew of the insurgent vessel, "Virginius," at Santiago de Cuba. Steaming for that port without orders, he stopped the executions, pending instructions from Spain by which they were entirely discontinued.

The following year, and the day before Cushing's untimely death (at Washington, December 17, 1874), the "Virginius" was handed over to the United States authorities. For three days, without medical attendance, the young commander had suffered indescribable tortures from sciatic inflammation. The servants in the house at last recognized the serious character of his ailment, and called a physician. Soon the inflammation reached the patient's brain, and he was removed to the government hospital for the insane, where, universally lamented, he expired some days later.

Of this young hero's personal appearance we have his own statement. In an early letter to his cousin he says that he was "tall and slim." In one of his published letters the poet Longfellow described his face as of a beauty resembling Schiller's. Since all of the foregoing was written, however, I have received from the widow of Commander Cushing (still living with their two daughters at Fredonia, New York), a letter containing a description of him so admirably lifelike that I am glad to reproduce it in full. For reasons appearing elsewhere, however, it would seem that her recollection of what she heard forty years ago as to Alonzo's stature is not so perfect as her remembrance of her husband. She writes under date of January 1, 1910:

Mr. Theron W. Haight,

MY DEAR SIR: Your letters of kind inquiry regarding Commander Cushing's personal appearance, height, etc., have unavoidably remained too long unanswered. I trust you will pardon the delay, and that the information I send will be satisfactory and not too late for your use.

I met Mr. Cushing for the first time in the late spring of 1867—a few months before I acted as bridesmaid at his sister's wedding.

Mr. Cushing was tall, slender and very erect. His movements easy and graceful, at the same time indicating force and strength. His head was well poised, his look clear, direct, and steady. His features were regular and clear cut, with a fascinating expression about the mouth when he smiled which attracted one's attention to that feature. His hair was of a medium brown, soft, fine, dark, and straight, without a suggestion of curl. His rather delicate mustache was of a lighter brown, suggestive of golden lights, never of reddish tints.

His animation and enthusiasm in conversation lent a glow to his light, blue-gray eyes that made them seem dark. His brilliant mind was expressed in choice and facile diction—he was a fluent and charming writer. All his impulses were fine, noble. He was generous to a fault, tender and affectionate, and exemplified the sentiment,

The bravest are the tenderest; The loving are the daring.

What he achieved and lived through in the Civil War, the perilous tasks he assumed and accomplished for his country in her time of greatest danger, form a background from which his figure stands out in vivid relief. It beams with his indomitable courage and is gilded with his heroic character.

I have often heard Mr. Cushing speak of his brother Alonzo, who was two years his senior and two inches taller. My husband was exactly six feet without shoes. They were as intimate and devoted as girls, and quite the opposite in manner and speech, I should say.

Alonzo and Howard I never saw, but the picture of the former stands out in my mind as a tall, gentle, dark-haired, reticent man (he was only 22 when he died), as against the younger, more lively and more impressionable brother.

When I became acquainted with Mr. Cushing, he seemed to have become the head of the family. I mean that he assumed and bore the responsibility of the family. He had been more fortunate in financial matters and was therefore in a position to help all the others, which he did on occasions with the most open-handed liberality.

WILLIAM BARKER CUSHING

From oil portrait (1865) by A. Bradish.

See Mrs. Cushing's letter, p. 87.

Alonzo died at Gettysburg in '63, long before I knew the family. Howard was killed by the Apaches after I was married. I well remember what a shock it was to my husband, and how he grieved for him, and tried to comfort his mother, obtaining all possible details of his brilliant service and lamentable death in Arizona through correspondence with the commanding general and officers, and with the War Department at Washington.

I wish to thank you most cordially for the fine photogravure you sent. It arrived in excellent condition. It is an admirable copy of the Bradish portrait, which we have, but the portrait itself does not seem correctly proportioned on the side turned away, being a trifle too broad under the eye, and so represents the face as too pointed. The photo shows it more clearly than the painting. My criticism of the portrait, however, does not affect your fine copy or the kindness that prompted you to send it. I thank you sincerely for it.

I wish also to thank you for the work you are doing, and trust your history of the *Three Wisconsin Cushings* will be admirable in every way, and fully meet your own expectations, as well as receive the merited reward of the approbation of the State Historical Society and of the public.

Respectfully yours,

KATE L. CUSHING.

FOREST PLACE, FREDONIA, N. Y.

Howard Cushing With the Artillery

Of Howard Cushing, the attainable memorials are very meagre. Indeed, whatever may have been the achievements of a private soldier in a volunteer regiment in war time, they are not commonly mentioned in official reports. In the case of Howard it is only apparent on the face of the records of the Illinois regiment with which he served, that his conduct there was at least sufficiently creditable to warrant his promotion (November 30, 1863) to a second lieutenancy in the regular artillery.

His claim to distinction was not made conspicuously emphatic during his artillery service. However, it is probable that this was due rather to circumstances than to any failure on his part to do what might be done by a soldier of very high class under the conditions which he found after entering the regular service. At his own request he was assigned to Battery A of the Fourth, in which his brother Alonzo lost his life. But he had not the éclat with which his brother was signalized on his graduation from West Point; moreover, the fact that Sergeant Fuger, now an officer in the same organization, had also served as an enlisted man, did not tend to keep it at the same level, in the esteem of other regular officers, as would have been the case had one of the two, at least, arrived at his position by way of the Academy. It may be that the exclusiveness here noted tends to the general advantage of the army, but not unlikely it is somewhat depressing to appointees from the ranks.

allow me to see home again for a few days, it will be a very happy time for me. Our campaign is ended and we are in Summer quarters, there is nothing down here for us to fight. Blair, our division commander, has gone up the river, and I don't know as he will command the division any more or not. Please to write to me at once, and tell me how things are working. I shall be very anxious. And, my dear brother, if I get the position it shall be my endeavor so to fill it, as to satisfy the government and my friends, and now with the hope of hearing from you soon, and with my best love to Will.

I REMAIN YOUR AFFEC. BROTHER HOWARD CUSHING

FACSIMILE OF PART OF LETTER FROM HOWARD B. CUSHING TO HIS BROTHER MILTON; DATED AUGUST 6, 1863

At all events, what happened to Battery A after Howard's assignment to duty with it was, that it was kept in camp near Brandy Station, Virginia, until the following March. Then it was attached to the second division of the cavalry corps of the Army of the Potomac, and took part in Sheridan's battles at Mine Run, Virginia (May 3, 1864), at Todd's Tavern (May 4), at Meadow Bridge (May 6), at Yellow Tavern, where General "Jeb" Stuart was killed in front of Howard's section (May 11), at Strawberry Hill (May 13), and at Hawes's Shop the same day. In these battles Howard commanded a section of two three-inch guns. The losses of the battery in those fights were so considerable that it was, in the latter part of May, sent back to Washington to recuperate, remaining there until after the conclusion of the war, with the exception hereinafter mentioned.

After its transfer to the capital, the last experience of the battery in hostilities came very near proving serious. Early's raid into Maryland occurred shortly after the first of July. On the ninth he fought a battle with a Union force on the Monocacy, in which he was victorious, and headed for Washington, then defended by only about 5,000 soldiers. Battery A was then at Fort Totten, near Bladensburg, where the ranking officer was a captain of one hundred-day troops from Ohio, and of course in command. He seems, nevertheless, to have had good discretion, and before making any movement in the way of defense requested the advice of the seasoned officers under him. Late on the tenth, soldiers of the Veteran Reserve Corps from the city, accompanied by clerks from the departments and convalescents from the hospitals, swarmed out to the outer line of earthworks and manned the rifle-pits stretching along between the forts.

The next day, Confederate cavalry came into sight and the smoke of burning houses behind them told the sort of work they were doing. In the afternoon, Confederate infantry appeared, but stopped after forming in line of battle. On the twelfth they began moving before sunrise, and were met by shells from the forts—among others, three 100-pound Parrott guns, handled by the men of Battery A, being brought into action. There was also infantry fighting, but not of a serious character. Towards night the Sixth Corps of the Union army, which had been brought up the river on transports, began to arrive at the earthworks, and no further danger was feared. Advancing in line of battle it was found that the Confederates were now in retreat; but if they had not been so cautious the day before, it is probable that Early's 18,000 tried soldiers would have made their way into Washington, and inflicted the most humiliating disaster of the war.

Late in the fall, the senior lieutenant of the battery being absent on leave, Lieutenant Cushing was ordered to take the men and guns to Elmira, New York, to assist in guarding the prison pen at that place. There, about 12,000 Confederates were confined, in charge of a regiment of short-term men, undisciplined and unaware of the responsibilities of their position. The prisoners were in consequence unruly and often uproarious.

The day after his arrival, Cushing went with his second in command, Lieutenant Frank Wilkeson, to inspect the outer lines of the camp, and was assailed with jeers and howls of contempt by the prisoners. Quick action was needed. Cushing gave the Confederates the following talk, reported[10] to have been delivered in a low, clear voice, in terms far from polite, but nevertheless effective, for no further trouble was experienced:

[10] Frank Wilkeson, *Recollections of a Private Soldier in the Army of the Potomac* (N. Y., 1887), pp. 223, 224.

See here ——, ——, ——! I am just up from the front, where I have been killing such infernal wretches as you are. I have met you in twenty battles. I never lost a gun to you. You never drove a battery I served with from its position. You are a crowd of insolent, cowardly scoundrels, and if I had command of this prison I would discipline you, or kill you, and I should much prefer to kill you. I have brought a battery of United States artillery to this pen, and if you give me occasion I will be glad to dam that river [pointing to the Chemung] with your worthless carcasses, and silence your insolent tongues forever. I fully understand that you are presuming on your position as prisoners of war when you talk to me as you have; but [and here his hand shook warningly in the faces of the group], you have reached the end of your rope with me. I will kill the first man of you who again speaks insultingly to me while I am in this pen, and I shall be here daily. Now, go to your quarters!

The release of all prisoners of war, in 1865, made unnecessary the further presence of cannon at Elmira. Cushing thereupon returned to Washington. His entire organization was dismounted, and early in 1866 assigned to duty as heavy artillery at Fort Meyer, across the river from Georgetown, D. C. It may well be imagined that the new service, consisting principally of drilling recruits, would not be much to the taste of the dashing young lieutenant who was now in his twenty-eighth year, full of life and vigor, a lover of literature and art, but above all imbued with the desire to write his name by the side of those of his brothers, whose services to their country were worthy of a permanent place on the tablets of the Nation's memory.

Transferred to the Cavalry

It was not until he had completed his twenty-ninth year that Howard obtained a transfer to the cavalry, which was then engaged in subduing Indians, the only warlike enterprise then in operation. On September 7, 1867, he became second-lieutenant of troop F of the Third cavalry, probably with reasonable certainty of early promotion, for about three months later he received a commission as first lieutenant.

ALONZO HERSFORD CUSHING

From the border annals, it would appear that thenceforward he was practically commander of his troop. So closely identified was he with it, that what the troop did was credited to Cushing, and what Cushing did was the pride and the boast of the troop. In captivating the hearts of his followers, Howard displayed a power and quality of bravery much resembling that of his brothers. Captain Bourke, who served with him as junior lieutenant, in the same troop, frankly stated in private conversation that Howard Cushing was the bravest man he ever saw; and repeated for emphasis, "I mean just that—the bravest man I ever saw." In Bourke's volume,[11] he writes to like effect, although not in the identical language above quoted. One among his many allusions to Cushing is given in the "Appreciations" preceding the present narrative; but there are others, expressed with nearly as strong emphasis—for instance, a list of the able and gallant officers who had helped clear Arizona of Apaches is recited, with the conclusion: "They were all good men and true, but if there were any choice among them I am sure that the verdict, if left to those soldiers themselves, would be in favor of Cushing." In a burst of indignation, after speaking of the lieutenant's "determination, coolness and energy, which had made his name famous all over the southwestern border," Bourke adds: "There is an alley named after him in Tucson, and there is, or was when last I saw it, a tumble-down, worm-eaten board to mark his grave, and that was all to show where the great American nation had deposited the remains of one of its bravest."

[11] John G. Bourke, *On the Border with Crook* (N. Y., 1891).

Cushing's first cavalry service of distinction was in western Texas, from which he drove the savages in 1869. The next spring, after a cruel massacre by the Indians of a party of thirty white men and women on their way to work at a private ranch, he was selected to head an expedition for the punishment of the murderers. Patiently searching for every indication of the trails of the Indians, he found their camp one night, and the following morning surprised and destroyed them, almost to the last man. They were said to have the more easily succumbed to the attack, from having drunk a quantity of patent medicines taken from the baggage of their earlier victims. This stuff was composed mostly of what the distillers call "high wines," containing a large percentage of crude alcohol.

On returning to Camp Grant the troop rested for a short time, and then started on an extended expedition touching the Sierra Apache and Mesquite Springs—losing only one man, the blacksmith, in the course of the trip, and inflicting no great injury on the Indians. Other expeditions followed, about as fruitless; but towards the end of summer the headquarters were moved fifty-five miles west to Tucson, which had not then acquired fame as a mining centre. It was, however, noted as being the capital of Arizona and one of the dirtiest of little Spanish-American towns. The camp was on the eastern border of the village, and the Apaches were in the habit of coming up to its close neighborhood to steal and drive away live stock. Even after the arrival of Cushing's troop, the savages had shown strong tendencies towards mischief, seriously wounding one of his men. Later they simultaneously attacked wagon trains and widely-separated settlements, thus confusing the calculations of our officers. As a crowning exploit they carried away a herd of cattle from Tucson itself, and followed that achievement by the killing of a stage-mail rider and the massacre of a party of Mexicans on their way to Sonora.

During the time when these events occurred, Cushing kept his troop hard at work and extirpated many of the hostile Indians—how many, is not stated in any work of which I have knowledge. Cochise, chief of the Chiricahua clan of Apaches (and predecessor of Geronimo), finally came into camp as winter drew nigh, and claimed that he wanted peace and a resting-place on the reservation. He had already been fighting the white people for fourteen years, and had tried every trick upon his enemies save this. Cushing vainly protested against coddling the wily chief during cold weather, to suffer from his depredations when warmth should again prevail. Cochise was taken care of all winter; and before May, 1871, was on the warpath with Cushing close after him. On May 5th the lieutenant was at the head of a reconnoitering party of twenty-two men at Bear Springs, in the Whetstone Mountains, about fifty miles southeasterly from Tucson, and twenty-five southwesterly from the site of the present town of Benson.

Death of the Young Cavalryman

Cushing was riding at the head of the party with three soldiers and a citizen or two near him, when Sergeant John Mott saw movements of some Apaches who were trying to get to the rear of the detachment. He sent word to the lieutenant, inducing him to fall back, although already engaged with an ambush of Cochise's followers in front. The latter had succeeded in entirely surrounding the little party, and Cushing, with four at his side, were all slain before they could get back to the rest of their party.

Sylvester Maury, a graduate of West Point—pioneer miner, and author of a classic of modern Arizona, entitled *Arizona and Sonora*—in a letter to the New York *Herald* shortly after Cushing's death, boldly charged the catastrophe to the foolish policy then prevailing, of dealing with the Indians of the Southwest. Under this policy, the ravages of the enemy were promoted by feeding them up well during any intervals when they might feel like taking a rest from assassination and plunder. He added:

Now we have the result. There is not a hostile tribe in Arizona or New Mexico, that will not celebrate the killing of Cushing as a great triumph. He was a beau sabreur, an unrelenting fighter; and although the Indians have got him at last, he sent before him a long procession of them to open his path to the undiscovered country. * * * He has left behind him in Arizona a name that will not die in this generation.

As a comment on the foregoing, I need only say that in response to my request, at an Arizona newspaper office a few weeks ago, for some special information regarding Howard Cushing, I was told that the writer had "never heard of the party inquired after." *Sic transit gloria mundi*, making very rapid time in the transit, in many of the modern instances. Nevertheless, Arizona has taken enough care of Cochise's name to attach it to one of her large counties.

Howard's death occurred more than three-and-a-half years before that of William; but I fancy that the acts and sayings of the latter at the time of his brother's demise were such as to indicate something in the nature of nervous affection. Mrs. Bouton informs me that it was difficult to dissuade him from a project that he had in mind, to go into the frontier service himself and there take vengeance on Howard's slayers. On first hearing of the fatality he had been unable to refrain from tears, even after reaching the office of a commercial bank. Before leaving the place, he wrote the following letter to his brother Milton:

THE BLACKSTONE NATIONAL BANK, BOSTON,

May 15th, 1871.

MY ONLY AND VERY DEAR BROTHER: With a heart full of agony I write to you of our terrible misfortune. Dear, brave "Howie" is no more. I saw the news in the paper at 8 a. m. in the country this morning, and hastened in to break it to Mother. Poor, dear little Ma! Her heart is almost broken. Oh! dear old fellow—we are left alone now—the last of four; and let us swear to stand by each other and our noble Mother in all things. Let our old boyhood and vows come back with full force and meaning, and let us cling together in truest and most unselfish love and friendship. I long for you, dear brother— for a clasp of your true, honest hand, and the comfort of one glance into your eyes. How much it would comfort Mother to see you before you go! Tomorrow I take her with me into the Country where we are living. I am in delightful quarters, and shall take good care of little Ma. God bless her! Kate [the writer's wife] is like a real daughter to her; and I thank Heaven that she was not alone in Mary's absence. [Referring to the present Mrs. Bouton, whose name was Mary Isabel, the "Mary" having since been dropped by her.]

Dear old fellow—we must be doubly loving and attentive to little Ma now. Write often to her. One thing is certain of her Sons; they can not be beaten. You can kill but not conquer them. A beautiful tribute was paid to Lon by the General of his brigade at the great Army of the Potomac meeting here. He described his wonderful, superhuman bravery. How he demanded— white with loss of blood—to go again to the front. The General said, "You have done all that mortal can do; attend now to your wounds." Lon answered, "No, I will fall by my guns." He selected Allie as the only one to especially eulogize, God bless the brave boys! I can almost see their meeting—the handclasp of two who gave up life for duty; and Father, joined by his noble Sons, proudly and tenderly embracing them.

God bless you, dear brother! Don't lose love for me. We are alone now. My tears are falling so that I can scarcely see. Good bye.

With all his heart your loving brother

WILL.

The story of these noble sons of Wisconsin might properly be concluded with the foregoing letter; but for the satisfaction of those who may wish to have a good idea of the personal appearance of the young cavalryman, I will add the description given by Captain Bourke:

He was about five feet seven in height, spare, sinewy, active as a cat; slightly stoop-shouldered, sandy complexioned, keen gray or bluish gray eyes, which looked you through when he spoke and gave a slight hint of the determination, coolness and energy which had made his name famous all over the southwestern border.

Kate is like a pal daughter to her and I thank Heaven that she was not alone in Macy's absence. Dear old fellow it must be doubly boring and attrition to little Ma now. Write often to her—One thing is certain of her Son—they can not be beaten. You care kill but not conquer them. A beautiful tribute was paid to Lon by the General of his brigade at the great Army of Potomac awaiting here. He described his wonderful, super human bravery. How he demanded—white with loss of blood—to go again to the front. The General said 'You have done all that mortal can do—attend now to your wounds.' Lon answered "No. I will fall by my guns." He selected Allie as the only one to especially eulogize. God bless the brave boys! I can almost see their meeting the hand clasp of two who gave up life for

- 50 -

duty, and Father, joined by his noble Sons proudly and tenderly embracing them.

God bless you—dear brother! Don't lose love for me—We are alone now—My tears are falling so that I can scarcely see—Good bye.

With all his heart

Your loving Brother

Will.

Facsimile of part of letter from William B. Cushing to his brother Milton; dated May 15, 1871

So long as such men can be produced in the republic, there is little danger of its decline and fall. Without such, or men of stamina approximating to their standard, our country would be likely to meet the fate of its predecessors, and become the prey of stronger peoples. It would therefore be foolish indeed to withhold from our fighting men the honor and the more substantial rewards which tend to encourage bravery and, when necessary, the upholding of our national solidarity by force of arms. To a considerable degree this is accomplished by our national pension system; but that is faulty, in respect that it makes no distinction, as to the amount of his quarterly stipend, between a four-years' fighting soldier and a ninety-days' malingerer in or about hospitals.

That it was difficult to provide for advancement in the army, in accordance with desert, is evident from the fact that Howard Cushing served as a private soldier in the same battery for twenty months. That was, indeed, keeping talent hidden in a very inconspicuous napkin. It may be that such bad fortune was unavoidable on the whole, and that a just grading of pensions would be still more difficult to attain than logically-just promotions in the army. At all events, it is clear to me that whatever does tend most effectually to keep alive in our citizenship such devotion to the country as to make men willing to strive to the uttermost and to die for its sake, is what ought to be practised— and where possible, improved.

9 789357 932684